As custodians of a priceless national heritage we are endeavouring to ensure
that this magnificent house and its treasures will be preserved for future
generations of visitors in these beautiful surroundings.
We very much hope that you will enjoy your visit.

Contents

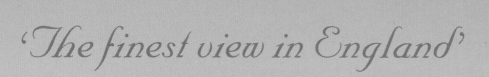

'The finest view in England'

"As we passed through the entrance archway and the lovely scenery burst upon me, Randolph said with pardonable pride, 'This is the finest view in England.' Looking at the lake, the bridge, the miles of magnificent park studded with old oaks, I found no adequate words to express my admiration and when we reached the huge and stately palace, I confess I felt awed."

Writing her reminiscences many years later, this is how Lady Randolph Churchill described her first impressions of Blenheim Palace in 1874. Today, Sir John Vanbrugh's magnificent baroque architecture and the beautiful landscape and lake of 'Capability' Brown inspire a similar feeling of awe in many of the thousands of modern-day visitors to Blenheim Palace.

Designated by the United Nations as a World Heritage Site, the Palace carries a unique aura of history and achievement. Blenheim Palace was the gift of Queen Anne and a grateful nation to the 1st Duke of Marlborough for his great victory at the Battle of Blenheim in 1704.

Everywhere the Palace's design reflects this triumphal mood, from the military details of the trophies on the colonnades to the scale of the heroic Grand Bridge. The dramatic effect harmonises perfectly with 'Capability' Brown's great lake and hanging beech woods beyond. It all looks so effortlessly natural but in fact the scene was artfully and laboriously created between 1764 and 1774. This is the view which Turner painted and which made George III exclaim: "We have nothing to equal this!"

History

The beginnings of Blenheim Palace

- Blenheim Palace is a supreme example of the style of architecture known as English Baroque.

- Vanbrugh saw Blenheim Palace much more as an intended monument to the Queen's glory than as a private habitation for the Duke of Marlborough.

John Churchill and his wife, Sarah, were already well established in royal circles at the time of Queen Anne's accession to the throne in March 1702. Sarah in particular was a close friend of the new Queen.

When war broke out in Europe later that year, Marlborough's extensive military experience made him the obvious choice of leader for the allied forces. The next two years saw Marlborough defending Holland from the French. Then, on 13 August 1704, he won a decisive victory at Blindheim or Blenheim, on the River Danube in Bavaria. The victory was a turning point in history, crushing Louis XIV's ambition to rule Europe. As Sir Winston Churchill memorably wrote: "The First Duke's victory at Blenheim changed the political axis of the world."

As a reward, Queen Anne granted Marlborough the Manor and Honour of Woodstock and the Hundred of Wootton, where a house would be built as a monument to his famous victory. John Vanbrugh, the architect of Castle Howard, was appointed to carry out the task but unfortunately the contract was never formalised.

The Great Court and north front, from an 18th century engraving

The family armorial bearing, from the East Gate

John, 1st Duke of Marlborough, the national hero, for whom the Palace was built, by John Closterman

Sarah, 1st Duchess of Marlborough, wearing a mantilla, thought to be in mourning, by Charles Jervas

This caused problems later, when the Queen's friendship with Sarah cooled and political plotting brought about Marlborough's fall from royal favour. Treasury payments for the building of Blenheim Palace dwindled. By 1712 the amount owing to Vanbrugh and others was £45,000 and all construction work ceased.

For the next two years the Marlboroughs lived abroad in self-imposed exile, only returning the day after Queen Anne died. Although the new King, George I, acknowledged the debt, no further Treasury money was forthcoming and the Duke decided to finish the Palace at his own expense, with Vanbrugh as architect and Nicholas Hawksmoor assisting him, as before.

Sir John Vanbrugh, the architect of Blenheim Palace, by Sir Godfrey Kneller

The building of Blenheim Palace

In his design for Blenheim Palace Vanbrugh's aim was to house a national hero and to celebrate England's newly won supremacy over the French in a blaze of architectural glory to rival Versailles. Its function, therefore, was to be a monument, castle, citadel and private house – in that order. As such, for the building Vanbrugh utilised all the mass ornamentation, symbolism and drama of the Baroque, following also contemporary conventions of symmetry and formality; for example, the typical arrangement of state rooms (ante-room, drawing room, bedroom) either side of a central saloon.

UNDER THE AUSPICES OF A MUNIFICENT SOVEREIGN THIS HOUSE WAS BUILT FOR JOHN DUKE OF MARLBOROUGH, AND HIS DUCHESS SARAH, BY SIR J. VANBRUGH BETWEEN THE YEARS 1705 AND 1722. AND THIS ROYAL MANOR OF WOODSTOCK; TOGETHER WITH A GRANT OF £240,000, TOWARDS THE BUILDING OF BLENHEIM WAS GIVEN BY HER MAJESTY QUEEN ANNE AND CONFIRMED BY ACT OF PARLIAMENT [3 & 4 ANNE C.4] TO THE SAID JOHN DUKE OF MARLBOROUGH AND TO ALL HIS ISSUE MALE AND FEMALE LINEALLY DESCENDING.

The inscription over the East Gate, by the 9th Duke

Although building work started again in 1716, at the 1st Duke's expense, he refused to pay Crown rates for the completion of the work and, as a result, master craftsmen such as Grinling Gibbons – who were still owed a considerable amount of money by the Treasury – never returned. Foreman-masons took over the work at the lower rates their masters refused to accept.

In November 1716, Vanbrugh too left in a rage. His ongoing differences with Duchess Sarah came to a head after her strong criticisms and "intolerable treatment" of him. The talented cabinet-maker, James Moore, took over supervision from Vanbrugh and Hawksmoor. The Duchess called him her "oracle" and praised his "understanding in many Trades besides his own". It was not until after the Duke's death in 1722, that Hawksmoor was recalled for the Triumphal Arch and other outworks but Vanbrugh remained in permanent disgrace. On one occasion, in 1725, while the Duchess was away, he managed to snatch a glimpse of the Palace but he was refused admittance even into the park. He died a year later.

• The inscription tells us that Blenheim Palace was built between 1705 and 1722 "under the auspices of a munificent sovereign". However, the Treasury contributed only £240,000 to the initial cost of the building; the Marlboroughs spent a further £60,000 completing it.

The lion of England assaults the cockerel of France

Trophies of war seen in front of the portico

The Clock Tower seen through the East Gate

The Clock Tower Arch with the lions of England and the cockerels of France, by Grinling Gibbons

The Great Hall

The magnificent 20-metre (67-foot) high Great Hall is one of Blenheim Palace's architectural glories. It is particularly outstanding for Sir James Thornhill's painted ceiling and its stone carvings "cutt extraordinry rich and sunk very deep" by Grinling Gibbons and his assistants, who also carved the sumptuous Corinthian capitals and the arms of Queen Anne on the keystone of the main arch. The latter spans a minstrels' gallery which was originally designed to open to the Saloon beyond.

In Thornhill's painting of 1716, the victorious 1st Duke of Marlborough is depicted in Roman garb kneeling in front of Britannia, presenting his plan of action at the Battle of Blenheim. Thornhill envisaged the Great Hall as a vast guard room – similar to those at Windsor and Hampton Court – full of dramatic suits of armour, pistols and swords. He went as far as sketching out his ideas, but they never came to fruition.

Above the Saloon door is a bust of the 1st Duke inscribed in Latin and English. The last line, "Nor cou'd Augustus better calm mankind", was felt by his Duchess, Sarah, "to bee an exact description of the Dear Duke of Marlboroughs temper". The hall doors feature a complicated lock, around which has grown a legend that it was copied from the original on the gates of Warsaw. It is accompanied by a huge, coroneted key.

The bronze bust of the 9th Duke in Garter robes is by Jacob Epstein. The Duke's cousin, Sir Shane Leslie, remarked that the bust captured his cousin's religious spirit: "as if it were a Quixote designed by Greco".

The elaborate lock in brass on the doors of the main entrance

The imposing Great Hall is 20 metres high

The 9th Duke of Marlborough, by Sir Jacob Epstein

The long corridors leading to the wings from the north and south sides of the Great Hall are typical of Vanbrugh. So too is the staircase concealed by the arcaded eastern wall. Good, simple ironwork supports the handrail and fronts the gallery. Originally a second staircase was planned behind the western wall.

Two white marble busts, of the 9th Duke and his Duchess, Consuelo, stand in the corridor leading from the Great Hall to the Long Library. They are the work of the American sculptor Waldo Story, who also produced the stunning Mermaid Fountain in the Italian Garden.

At the suggestion of Sir Winston Churchill, the artist Paul Maze, who has several of his paintings on display at the Palace, gave the splendid collection of lead soldiers to the present Duke of Marlborough at Christmas 1935. Sir Winston's painting of the Great Hall (1928) can be seen in the Churchill Exhibition. In recent years, as part of the rewiring of the palace, the lighting in the Great Hall has been enhanced.

The striking view from the Great Hall through the front door to the Column of Victory

- Symbolically, the north-south axis of the Palace connects the Column of Victory of the 1st Duke to the north, with the grave of Sir Winston Churchill to the south.

The Waldo Story busts of the 9th Duke and Duchess, Consuelo, in the North Corridor

14

The Great Hall ceiling, painted by Sir James Thornhill. Marlborough kneels to Britannia and proffers a plan of the Battle of Blenheim

Sir Winston Churchill

On 30 November 1874, Lady Randolph Churchill gave birth to Winston Churchill in a small bedroom just off the Great Hall, in the former apartments of Dean Jones, the 1st Duke's chaplain. Blenheim Palace's most famous son was later to write: "At Blenheim I took two very important decisions: to be born and to marry. I am happily content with the decisions I took on both those occasions."

Today Sir Winston Churchill's Birth Room and the Churchill Exhibition nearby are a major attraction for visitors to the Palace. Among the items on show in the Birth Room are the young Winston Churchill's curls, and next door, the maroon, velvet siren suit he wore during his long nights on duty during the Second World War, a pair of monogrammed slippers and the original of 'The Budget', Sir Max Beerbohm's celebrated cartoon of 1910.

"At Blenheim I took two very important decisions: to be born and to marry"

In it, Churchill is reassuring his cousin, the 9th Duke: "There is nothing in the budget to make it harder for a poor hardworking man to keep a small home in decent comfort." The small home in the background is, of course, Blenheim Palace!

• A national hero, Sir Winston Churchill (1874–1965) was elected to parliament in 1900 and held a number of important ministerial posts over the next 55 years. He was Britain's Prime Minister 1940–45 and 1951–55. Created a Knight of the Garter in 1953, he was also a prolific author and artist and was voted 'Greatest Briton of All Time' in BBC Television's recent survey.

Sir Winston Churchill by Clare Sheridan

Blenheim Palace was a rich resource for Sir Winston, the painter

Sir Winston Churchill's painting of the Great Hall

Sir Winston Churchill at Blenheim Palace in 1958

In his youth, Winston Churchill spent many happy days at Blenheim Palace at the Oxfordshire Yeomanry camps in the Park with the 9th Duke and their mutual friend 'F E' Smith, later Lord Birkenhead. After training there would be parties in the Palace or card games in each other's tents.

In 1908, Winston Churchill persuaded his cousin, the 9th Duke, to invite Clementine Hozier to stay at the Palace. Winston proposed to her on 11th August in the Temple of Diana in the grounds, where the couple had taken shelter from a summer downpour. A plaque now commemorates the event.

They spent the first days of their honeymoon at Blenheim Palace and remained frequent visitors to the Palace, despite the political differences between Winston (then a radical Liberal) and the Duke (a staunch Tory). Blenheim Palace was to prove an inspiration to Churchill, not only for his paintings but also in his sense of history; for example, when he was researching his ancestor for the biography, Marlborough, His Life and Times, published in the 1930s.

In later years Winston Churchill continued to be a regular visitor to the Palace. In 1947, during his years in opposition, he spoke at a major political rally on the South Lawn and, in 1953, as Prime Minister, he was among the guests at the Blenheim Palace Commonwealth Garden Party for the Coronation, which was attended by Princess Margaret.

Sir Winston Churchill's curls

SIR WINSTON CHURCHILL'S CURLS
Cut from his head when he was five years old.

Churchill's painting of the West Front of Blenheim Palace (painted early 1920s) before the building of the Water Terrace

WINSTON
LEONARD
SPENCER
CHURCHILL
1874 - 1965
CLEMENTINE
OGILVY
SPENCER
CHURCHILL
1885 - 1977

In the Churchill Exhibition, near the Birth Room, there is a bronze of Sir Winston and Lady Churchill by Oscar Nemon. Churchill's picture of the Great Hall hangs nearby, a gift to the 10th Duchess. Other exhibits include a collection of his private letters and a piece of shrapnel which, in the First World War, fell between himself and his cousin, the 9th Duke. As the inscription points out, the shrapnel might easily have prevented their lifelong friendship.

The grave of Sir Winston Churchill, who was buried in St Martin's Churchyard, Bladon January 1965

- Sir Winston Churchill did not begin to paint until he was 41 years old. He was given his first paints by his brother Jack's wife, Lady Gwendolen.

19

West and South Corridors

As you pass through the Great Hall you will see Closterman's large painting of the 1st Duke and Duchess, their four daughters and their son, the 1st Marquis of Blandford, who died of smallpox at the age of 17. The painting dates from 1697. After the 1st Duke's death in 1722, his eldest daughter, Henrietta, became Duchess in her own right. When she died in 1733, the dukedom passed to Charles, son of Anne Spencer, Countess of Sunderland (wearing red in the painting). His younger brother, John, was the ancestor of the Earls Spencer.

The scrolled brackets supporting the gallery were beautifully carved by Grinling Gibbons and his assistants.

In the China Ante Room, outside the Green Drawing Room, are displays of Meissen (Dresden) and Sèvres porcelain. The Meissen, with its distinctive 'sliced-lemon' handles on the tureens, was presented to the 3rd Duke by the King of Poland who was then given a pack of staghounds by the Duke.

Consuelo, 9th Duchess of Marlborough, by Ambrose McEvoy

The 1st Duke and Duchess of Marlborough with their family, by John Closterman

A Meissen tureen, part of a service presented to the 3rd Duke by the King of Poland

The China Ante Room

The Green Drawing Room. Over
the chimneypiece is the portrait of
the 4th Duke by George Romney

Caroline, 4th Duchess of Marlborough, dancing her baby on her knee, by Sir Joshua Reynolds

- Towards the end of his life the 4th Duke became a virtual recluse. He declined to receive Lord Nelson and the Hamiltons when they called in 1802. He died in 1817.

- The 4th Duke was an ardent astronomer and was presented with a Herschel telescope by his lifelong friend George III in 1786, when the king visited Blenheim Palace and made his celebrated remark: "We have nothing to equal this!"

The original ceilings in the Green Drawing Room, the Red Drawing Room and the Green Writing Room show an innovative combination of coving and banding, which creates a powerful effect of height and might. They are the work of Nicholas Hawksmoor, Vanbrugh's collaborator, who had worked under Sir Christopher Wren and who was amongst the best-trained professional architects of his day.

Green Drawing Room

Fine portraits in the Green Drawing Room include two of the 1st Duchess. In Jervas' portrait she is seen wearing a mantilla (possibly in mourning) and in the other, by Kneller, she is depicted playing cards with Lady Fitzharding.

The Romney over the chimneypiece is of George Spencer, the 4th Duke, who succeeded to the title in 1758. A painting by Reynolds on the north wall shows his Duchess, Caroline, and her baby. It was the 4th Duke, with the inspired help of architect Sir William Chambers and landscape designer 'Capability' Brown, who added significantly to the beauty of Blenheim Palace both inside and out.

The elaborate mirror was made for the 4th Duke by Ince and Mayhew; the ornate clock, mounted upon a black bull, is by Gosselin of Paris.

Rococo pier glass by Ince and Mayhew. The clock is Louis XVIth, by Gosselin of Paris

Red Drawing Room

The two large paintings facing each other in this room create a deliberate contrast for dramatic effect. On the right-hand wall hangs Sir Joshua Reynolds' 1778 portrait of the 4th Duke of Marlborough and his family. Many of the children were keen amateur actors; they performed in a sumptuous private theatre in the Orangery, which contained seating for 200–300 people. Audiences were drawn from the county neighbours and the 'town and gown' of Oxford. Reynolds' lively group shows the connoisseur 4th Duke in his Garter robes, holding a sardonyx from his gem collection. His heir, the Marquis of Blandford (later the 5th Duke), carries a box containing more of the gems, while in the centre Lady Charlotte is depicted teasing their four-year-old sister, Lady Anne, who told Reynolds when she first saw him, "I won't be painted!" The story goes that Reynolds was determined to capture her look of fear, hence the mask charade.

It is said that the artist, while painting the family group at the Palace, dropped snuff on the carpet. The Duchess immediately sent for a footman to clear it up but Reynolds dismissed him, saying, "the dust you make will do more harm to my picture than my snuff to the carpet!"

The 9th Duke and Duchess of Marlborough and their two sons, by John Singer Sargent

Opposite is John Singer Sargent's stylish portrait of the 9th Duke and his family, painted in 1905. Like his ancestor, the Duke is attired in Garter robes, while his wife, Consuelo – at Sargent's suggestion – wore "a black dress whose wide sleeves were lined with deep rose satin", modelled on the dress Lady Killigrew is wearing in the painting by Van Dyck, which also hangs in this room.

Fame by Antoine Coysevox

For many years this room was used by the family as a Billiards room

Lady Killigrew and a lady called the 'Countess of Morton' by Sir Anthony Van Dyck

The 4th Duke and Duchess of Marlborough and their family, by Sir Joshua Reynolds

The chimneypiece was executed by Joseph Wilton to a design by Sir William Chambers, who also probably designed the mahogany doors along this front. Much admired by George III, the architect was brought in by the 4th Duke to embellish Blenheim Palace in the 1760s. He was responsible for the redecoration of several rooms and for embellishments to the East (Flagstaff) Gate, as well as for the 'New' Bridge over the Glyme on the south side of the park and the Temple of Diana in the grounds.

The central plaque of the chimneypiece depicts the marriage of Cupid and Psyche, a reference to one of the Marlborough gems. This collection was sold in 1875. Above the fireplace hangs Van Dyck's portrait of Margaret Lemon, shown as Erminia.

The room also contains large bronzes of Fame and Mercury by Coysevox (1640–1720), while, amongst the small bronzes on the mantelshelf is 'Ganymede' by Soldani (1656–1740).

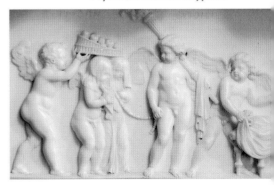

The marriage of Cupid and Psyche on the chimneypiece

Green Writing Room

Sir Winston Churchill, father of the 1st Duke of Marlborough, English School

A grenadier takes a French royal standard as a spoil of war

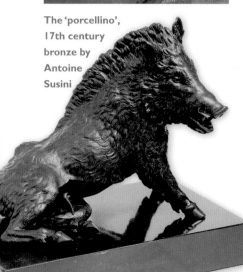

The 'porcellino', 17th century bronze by Antoine Susini

Taking pride of place in the Green Writing Room is the famous Blenheim tapestry, showing Marlborough in his hour of triumph as he accepts Marshal Tallard's surrender after the Battle of Blenheim (1704). The French, who had imagined they were invincible, turned and fled humiliated from the battlefield, many of them straight into the Danube. At home, Marlborough's feat was greeted as the greatest military victory since Agincourt; his genius as military commander had saved Europe from French domination. A grateful nation built him his great house, Blenheim Palace, as a suitable monument, on the Royal Manor of Woodstock that Queen Anne had granted him. Marlborough had also saved the Holy Roman Empire of the Hapsburgs and as his reward he was made a Prince of the Empire by Emperor Leopold and given the Principality of Mindelheim in Swabia by the Emperor Joseph.

The Blenheim tapestry, commissioned by the 1st Duke himself, is a superb example of the weaver's art. The details have an eye-witness authenticity. For example, behind the grenadier with the captured French standard one can see a field dressing-station, watermills ablaze, the village of Blindheim full of French troops and, in the far distance, the allies pursuing the enemy into the Danube. The captured Marshal Tallard was sent to England and kept prisoner at Nottingham, where he was handsomely treated. In fact he was far better treated than Marlborough himself who, despite his heroism, was dismissed by Queen Anne in 1711.

The tapestry hanging opposite the Blenheim tapestry shows an incident at Wynendael (1708), where a sergeant with his halberd seems needed to keep the hired driver of a 'Marlbrouk' military cart at his post.

The portrait over the chimneypiece is of Elizabeth, 3rd Duchess of Marlborough, by Van Loo and studio.

A portrait of the 1st Duke by Closterman hangs to the right of the chimneypiece. It is said that towards the end of his days the Duke stopped in front of this portrait of himself in his prime and murmured: "This was once a man."

Boulle pedestal clock, c. 1740. Signed Benj. Gray and J. Vulliamy

The 1st Duke receives the surrender of Marshal Tallard

- The silk damask wallcovering in the Green Writing Room has been renewed by the present Duke and features a family coat of arms.

Saloon

This is the state dining room, now used by the family only once a year, on Christmas Day. The table is elegantly laid, often to show the year's seasonal changes. The large, silver centrepiece by Garrard, standing on a separate table, shows Marlborough, still on horseback after his victory at the Battle of Blenheim, writing his famous dispatch. A copy is now displayed in the First State Room.

Sir James Thornhill, the artist responsible for the magnificent ceiling painting in the Great Hall, was originally commissioned to paint the Saloon and actually produced a number of carefully finished drafts, but he had fallen out with the 1st Duchess over his fee for the Great Hall ceiling. Indeed, she suspected him of sharp

The Saloon ceiling, by Louis Laguerre

practice in charging 25 shillings (£1.25) a yard for the murals in grisaille – which she considered "not worth half-a-crown (12.5p) a yard" – as well as for the "historical part" (ceiling) in colour. In the event, the French artist, Louis Laguerre (1663–1721), received the commission and charged £500 for the whole room. Various nations of the world are represented in the wall paintings, while the ceiling shows the 1st Duke in victorious progress but stayed by the hand of Peace. Laguerre's portrait of himself (above his signature on the west wall) can be seen beside Dean Jones, the 1st Duke's chaplain, whom the Duchess tolerated because he made her husband laugh and shared his fondness for cards.

Over the doors the 1st Duke's armorial bearing, including the black double-headed eagle – the crest of the Holy Roman Empire of which he was a Prince – is emblazoned. Only one of the four marble doorcases commissioned from Grinling Gibbons had been completed by 1712, when building operations ground to a halt. Although work resumed in 1716, the master carver never returned.

From the Saloon portico it is possible to see the site of the Great Parterre, now the South Lawn, and, beyond that, Bladon Church, where Sir Winston Churchill, his wife and his parents are buried. It was from this portico that Churchill addressed an audience of 40,000 at a Conservative Party rally in August 1947.

From the murals on the Saloon walls: a self-portrait of Laguerre with Dean Jones, the 1st Duke's chaplain

The armorial bearing of the 1st Duke

Silver centrepiece of Marlborough on horseback after his victory at Blenheim, writing his famous dispatch to his Duchess

• In the 1930s the number of 'under stairs' staff at the Palace included a butler, under-butler, groom of the chambers, three or four footmen, two odd-job men, a housekeeper, half a dozen housemaids, two still-room maids, a chef and six or so kitchen staff. The footmen were still liveried at this time and their duties included wafting scent, contained in long rods, around the rooms. The electric bulbs were also fitted with scent-filled asbestos rings.

The Saloon is still used by the family on Christmas Day

First State Room

The three rooms connecting the Saloon and the Long Library on the south front are known as the First, Second and Third State Rooms.

The walls of all three rooms are hung with tapestries showing Marlborough's battles and are part of a sequence of eleven tapestries he commissioned from the designer, de Hondt, and the weaver, de Vos, to depict his major victories. They are outstanding in their realistic detail.

The Donauwörth tapestry on the right-hand wall of the First State Room, next to the Saloon, depicts Marlborough preparing to storm the hilltop fortress. In the foreground, dragoons have loaded their horses with fascines (bundles of sticks) to help the infantry cross the enemy's defences. In the background, the walled city of Donauwörth prepares its defences.

Other tapestries in this room portray the Battle of Malplaquet (1709), the crossing of the Lines of Brabant and the Siege of Lille. Malplaquet was considered an allied victory, even though there were 22,000 allied casualties, compared with only 11,000 French.

A copy of Marlborough's famous dispatch from the Blenheim battlefield to his Duchess, Sarah, is on display in the First State Room. The dispatch, which he scribbled on the back of a tavern bill – the only piece of paper to hand – asks his wife to tell the Queen "that her army has had a glorious victory". The original, along with other Marlborough papers, is held in the British Library.

Also on display here is a Quit-rent standard, a French royal standard with its three *fleurs-de-lys*. By order of Queen Anne a new standard is presented to the sovereign on every anniversary of the Battle of Blenheim. Although the battle was fought on 2nd August, owing to later changes in the calendar the modern date is 13th August.

Silver and gilt 'Tula' bronze vase. Russian, late 18th/19th century

Quit-rent standard presented to the sovereign as 'rent' for Blenheim Palace

The Blenheim Dispatch

• The ornate cradle in which Duchess Consuelo, the 9th Duchess, rocked her two sons.

An Italian cradle given to the 9th Duchess by her mother

• In the Second World War
  the State Rooms became
  temporary classrooms,
  when pupils from Malvern
  College were evacuated
  to Blenheim Palace at the
  10th Duke's suggestion.

Second State Room

An imposing portrait of the Sun King, Louis XIV, hangs above the chimneypiece. In 1673 the 1st Duke, then Captain John Churchill, served in the Royal English Regiment of the French army, England's ally against the Dutch at that time. After the Siege of Maastricht, the young captain was personally thanked by Louis XIV. He was offered promotion to the rank of colonel in the French army and fought in Alsace and southern Germany under the brilliant commander Henri, Vicomte de Turenne. However, when the War of the Spanish Succession started in 1702, the former allies were on opposing sides. Following Marlborough's decisive victory at Blenheim, when French invincibility of 60 years was brought to a crushing end, it is said Le Roi Soleil banned any further mention of the battle in his presence.

Flanking this portrait hang tapestries representing Marlborough's siege of Bouchain including the penetration of Marshal Villar's vaunted ne plus ultra ('unsurpassable') lines in 1711. These were woven in Brussels under the 1st Duke's careful supervision. The dog in the Bouchain tapestry appears to have been given horse's hooves!

The furniture in the Second State Room includes commodes by Migeon and candelabra by Matthew Boulton made from blue-john (a banded variety of fluorite found in Derbyshire). There are some fine bronzes, including one of Hercules and the Centaur made in Italy in the 17th century. The baby in bronze, later the 10th Duke, is by Emil Fuchs.

Through the door from the First State Room (Robert, 2nd Earl of Sunderland, grandfather of the 3rd Duke, after Sir Godfrey Kneller) showing a lady, possibly Henrietta, 2nd Duchess, attributed to Charles Jervas

From a Bouchain tapestry, the detail shows a dog with what appear to be horse's hooves

Hercules and the Centaur, 17th century Italian bronze

One of a pair of blue-john and ormolu candelabra by Matthew Boulton

The Kakiemon vase

Bronze of the Scythian slave, French, c. 1700

Louis XIVth Boulle coffer by
Andre Charles Boulle, c. 1685

Third State Room

The Third State Room was originally the state bedchamber and features magnificently ornate Boulle furniture; the carpet is a Savonnerie.

On the centre of the mantelpiece is a Kakiemon vase, a very fine piece of Japanese porcelain of the late 17th century.

Above the fireplace is Enoch Seeman's portrait of Marlborough studying a plan of Bouchain with his chief military engineer, Colonel Armstrong. The first Duchess once remarked to the Duchess of Bedford: "I really think that picture of your grandfather with Mr Armstrong as like him as I ever saw and he [Seeman] was so humble as to ask me 17 guineas (£17.85) for both figures." Colonel Armstrong was later commissioned by the first Duchess to construct the Park's water features from the original stream. This canal system that ran under the bridge was subsequently lost when 'Capability' Brown built the Lake.

The large tapestry on the north wall shows a victorious Marlborough at Oudenarde (1708). Marlborough and his comrade-in-arms, Prince Eugène, overwhelmed an enormous French force under the incompetent command of the Dukes of Vendôme and Burgundy. After this battle an opportunity for peace in Europe was missed when Louis XIV hinted that a treaty might be acceptable, only to reject the terms that were subsequently offered. A bloodbath ensued at Malplaquet in 1709. After the battle Marlborough is said to have drunk from the Venetian glass goblet displayed in the case to the right.

The 'Kneeling Venus' by Coysevox, on the mantelpiece, is one of several outstanding bronzes in the room.

**Bronze bust of the 1st
Duke, 19th century, on a
Boulle pedestal**

**Detail showing Boulle's
fine, intricate work in
brass and tortoiseshell**

Long Library

"This gallery, from one part or other of it shows everything worth seeing about the seat," said Vanbrugh, describing the views from the Long Library, which runs the length of the west front. Vanbrugh built the Palace from east to west, so that the family could live in the east wing while the house was being finished. The Long Library was one of the last rooms to be decorated.

Originally planned by Vanbrugh as a "noble room of parade" or picture gallery, it measures 56 metres (183 feet) long and 10 metres (32 feet) high. It is considered to be Nicholas Hawksmoor's finest room at Blenheim Palace. Hawksmoor approached the design as if it were a sequence of five rooms, rather than a single long one. After he left, the work was completed according to his design. The architect's anxiety about how the great room would be finished is evident in his letters of 1722–25 to the 1st Duchess, for example: "ther's none can judg so well of the designe as the person who composed it, therefore I should beg leave to take a Convenient time to Slip downe …".

The style of the marble doorcase, erected between 1723 and 1725, also reveals Hawksmoor's talent. As Vanbrugh's biographer, Laurence Whistler, has commented: "Though Blenheim as a whole is Vanbrugh's, yet there is not one detail of which one could say with certainty that Hawksmoor had not designed it."

Originally planned by Vanbrugh as a 'noble room of parade' or picture gallery

One of the decorated window arches

The statue of Queen Anne by John Michael Rysbrack

- The Long Library has been put to a variety of uses in its lifetime, including serving as a hospital ward during the First World War and as a dormitory (duly boarded and protected) for Malvern College boys during the Second World War.

- The Library was Sir Winston Churchill's favourite room.

- The Library is said to be the second longest room in any house in England.

- From 1940–44 the Long Library was full of desks used by clerks of MI5.

Shelves showing part of the collection of volumes by, and about, Sir Winston Churchill

One of the internal ceiling domes showing the quality of Isaac Mansfield's stucco work

The superb stucco decoration of the ceiling, including two internal domes, was created by Isaac Mansfield in 1725. However, the ceiling panels, which appear to float on a sea of stucco, remain blank. Sir James Thornhill had been commissioned to paint them with allegorical scenes, but the 1st Duchess had already refused to pay his rates. The famous 'Sunderland Library' was housed in this room from 1744 until its sale in 1881–82. The present library of 10,000 volumes was collected by the 9th Duke.

Part of Hawksmoor's marble door case

The Library, showing an
interesting late 18th century
German bureau à cylindre

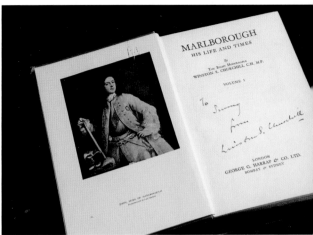

A first edition of Sir Winston Churchill's biography of
the 1st Duke, signed by the author

The bound correspondence of the 7th Duke
as Viceroy of Ireland

The statue of Queen Anne and the bust of Marlborough, both by Rysbrack, were commissioned by Sarah. She wrote in 1735: "I am going to Rysbrack to make a bargain with him for a fine statue of Queen Anne, which I will put up in the bow window room with a proper inscription. It will be a very fine thing and though but one figure will cost me £300, I have a satisfaction in showing this respect to her, because her kindness to me was real. And what happened afterwards was compassed by the contrivance of such as are in power now." Rysbrack's bust of Marlborough stands in the central bay on a pedestal designed by Sir William Chambers.

Portraits of Queen Anne, King William III and the 1st Duke hang on the east wall, together with paintings of three of the Duke's daughters: Elizabeth, Countess of Bridgewater; Anne, Countess of Sunderland (from whom the Earls Spencer and later Dukes of Marlborough descend); and Mary, Duchess of Montagu.

"In memory of happy days and as a tribute to this glorious home we leave thy voice to speak within these walls in years to come when ours are still."

The organ console finished in Italy at a cost of £400

1st Duke, by John Michael Rysbrack, on a pedestal designed by Sir William Chambers

The Willis organ at the north end of the Library, which originally stood in the central bay, was moved to its present position in 1902. It was installed by the 8th Duke and his American Duchess, Lilian, in 1891. When the Duke died the following year, this moving inscription for the front of the organ was found scribbled on a piece of paper torn from The Times: "In memory of happy days and as a tribute to this glorious home we leave thy voice to speak within these walls in years to come when ours are still."

The central bay contains the coronation robes worn by the 10th Duke and Duchess for the coronations of King George VI and the present Queen, the coronets of the 9th Duke and Duchess, various liveries and a cap worn by Queen Anne.

The organ, Henry Willis, 1891

- Sarah insisted on simplicity in the rest of the Chapel in order to emphasise the importance of her husband's monument. "Considering how many wonderful figures and whirligigs I have seen architects finish a chappel … that are no manner of use but to laugh at … what I have designed for this chappel may as reasonably be called finishing of it as pews or pulpit." Sarah's aim for the Chapel was obscured in Victorian times.

- In the 9th Duke's day, at the turn of the 20th century, a bell would toll for prayers at 9.30 am, when servants would stop in mid-chore and rush to take their places in the Chapel on time.

The Chapel from the upper entrance, which was originally the family pew

On either side of the sarcophagus are large statues representing History, with her quill, and Fame, with her trumpet. Beneath it, Envy is crushed.

Vanbrugh's original orientation of the Chapel was altered by the 1st Earl of Godolphin, a friend of the Marlboroughs, who placed the high altar on the west. Further alterations took place in the 19th century when the original marble pulpit was sent to Waddesdon church and the old pews to a Combe chapel. All the Chapel furnishings – organ, woodwork and marble-balustraded steps – are Victorian additions. On the south wall stands a statue of Lord Randolph Churchill, father of Sir Winston Churchill.

Chapel

The Chapel is dominated by the dramatic monument to the 1st Duke (dressed as a Roman general) and Duchess and their two sons, both of whom died young. Their four daughters are not included in the family group. The marble monument, which cost £2,200, was designed by William Kent and sculpted by Rysbrack at the Duchess's direction. As the monument's theme, Sarah chose to portray her husband as a victorious hero. She declared herself satisfied with the tomb and its "Marble Decorations of figures, Trophies, Medals with their inscriptions and in short, everything that could do the Duke of Marlborough Honour and Justice." As the Chapel was not finished when Marlborough died in 1722, he was buried in Westminster Abbey and re-interred here with Sarah after her death in 1744.

The Sovereign's Standard of the Life Guards laid up in the Chapel 16 May 2004

Rybrack's monument to the 1st
Duke and Duchess and their two
sons, both of whom died young

BLENHEIM PALACE

The Untold Story

300 YEARS *of* ENTICING TALES

A fascinating visitor experience "Blenheim Palace: The Untold Story - 300 years of enticing tales" is open on the first floor of the Palace where you can discover a whole new perspective on the history of Blenheim Palace.

"Blenheim Palace: The Untold Story" offers a world of unique and fascinating perspectives as you meet the ghost of Grace Ridley, beloved ladies maid to the first Duchess of Marlborough, who will guide you beneath the glamour and grandeur of the Palace and reveal its hidden history.

Follow Grace as she tells some of the lesser known stories about Britain's Greatest Palace and its fascinating inhabitants. See Grinling Gibbons struggle under the weight of stone carvings as Grace tells of the wilful 1st Duchess, and her demands on the building of the Palace, the 1st Duke's affair with the mistress of King Charles II, and the 8th Duke's pioneering scientific experiments. Interactive audio-visual exhibits provide more information about the illustrious Marlborough family seen through the eyes of the household staff.

Park and Gardens

Sometimes, when a new house is built, the design of the grounds is left until later, but not at Blenheim Palace. "The Garden Wall was set agoing the Same day with the House," Vanbrugh reported to the 1st Duke shortly after the Palace's foundation stone was laid in 1705. From the start Marlborough showed a strong personal interest in the construction of Blenheim Palace's gardens. His gardener, Henry Wise, realising that the Duke might not live to see the garden in its maturity (in fact he only spent two summers at the Palace), transplanted full-grown trees in baskets to achieve the desired early maturity. Following the fashion at that time, Wise decreed that everything within sight of the house should be formal, regular and symmetrical.

The Palace across 'Capability' Brown's lake with Vanbrugh's bridge

Tastes changed later in the 18th century and much of Vanbrugh and Wise's splendid original park and gardens were 'naturalised' by 'Capability' Brown. His picturesque approach was to present a landscape that appeared natural but was in fact nature contrived to pleasing effect. Brown realised the 'capabilities' of Blenheim Palace by creating the sublime lake and cunningly planned vistas with ornamental clumps and fringes of trees.

At the start of the last century, however, the 9th Duke decided to give Vanbrugh's Palace the formal setting he thought it deserved. Between 1900 and 1910, with the help of the French landscape architect, Achille Duchêne (an admirer of Louis XIV's great landscapist, Le Nôtre), he undertook the enormous task of restoring the 1.2 hectare (3-acre) forecourt, which had been grassed over by Brown, with cobbles and gravel. He also renovated the entire gardens on the east and west fronts, resulting in the Italian Garden and the magnificent Water Terraces.

The Water Terraces

- Sir Winston Churchill wrote of Blenheim Palace: "The cumulative labours of Vanbrugh and 'Capability' Brown have succeeded at Blenheim in setting an Italian palace in an English park without apparent incongruity."

- In the 10th Duke's time there were at least 30 people working in the Palace gardens and the number did not decrease significantly until the 1960s.

Undoubtedly the majestic Water Terraces on the west front are a major part of the 9th Duke's outstanding legacy to the Palace. A remarkable 20th century achievement, they have been compared to the Parterre d'Eau at Versailles. The Duke took his inspiration from Bernini whose river-gods fountain, now on the lower terrace, is a scale model of the original in Rome's Piazza Navona.

The caryatids and tiered shells between the Water Terraces

On the South Front: the Dying Gaul

A corner of the Upper Water Terrace

- Duchêne had envisaged the water in the terraces to be in perpetual motion, but was overruled by the 9th Duke, who insisted: "Limpidity of water is pleasing and possesses a romance."

- In 1933, the year before his death, the 9th Duke described the gardens at the East and West Fronts as "in perfect architectural design: a worthy frame to the Palace".

The 9th Duke commissioned Achille Duchêne to build the Water Terraces between 1925 and 1930. The two terraces are linked by a wall of caryatids, carved in situ by Visseau and flanked by tiers of shells. The head and torso of the northernmost (i.e. extreme left) caryatid are modelled on one of the gardeners, a local man, Bert Timms of Hanborough, who happened to walk by one day as Visseau was working.

The perfect Grecian features of Gladys, the 9th Duke's second Duchess, adorn the faces of a pair of sphinxes that face each other on the lower terrace. Made in 1930, they were modelled in lead by H. Ward Willis.

In 1929, when the work was virtually complete, the 9th Duke wrote: "Pray tell Monsieur Duchêne that the ensemble of the terraces is magnificent and in my judgement far superior to the work done by Le Nôtre at Versailles. The proportion of the house, the terrace and the lake is perfect."

One of two sphinxes guarding the third terrace. The head of each sphinx is that of Gladys Deacon, second wife of the 9th Duke

The symmetry of the Water Terraces

51

- The Italian Garden was built on the site of the 1st Duchess's flower garden, which was originally enclosed by Vanbrugh's 'out-boundary wall'. The Duchess objected that the latter spoilt her view from the bow window and it was demolished.

The Mermaid Fountain by Waldo Story in the Italian Garden

The Italian Garden

When the 9th Duke succeeded to the title in 1892 he wasted no time in commissioning the French landscape architect, Achille Duchene, to create an Italian Garden to adorn the east front of the Palace.

The garden enjoys a delightful, sheltered position, bordered on two sides by the Orangery and the East Front. Despite its name, the Italian Garden would not look out of place at a French château. With its precise, evergreen topiary, patterned beds, luscious orange trees and the scented pink blooms of the rose 'Caroline Testout', it is beautiful in all seasons. As a centrepiece it has the stunning, gilded Mermaid Fountain by the American sculptor, Waldo Story.

The Italian Garden and East Front

The tranquillity of the Secret Garden

The Secret Garden

As part of the commemoration of the tercentenary in 2004 of the Battle of Blenheim, the present Duke restored this garden, first laid down by his father, keeping much of the original layout while introducing many new features.

As a 'garden for all seasons', the mature and new plantings create interest throughout the year.

In contrast to the formal gardens and sweeping parkland it is a secluded area where winding paths lead over bridges to tranquil water, ponds and streams. Its style and the fact that the plants are named means visitors can relate this to their own gardens.

The Arboretum

From the Water Terraces a walk leads southwards past the Temple of Diana, built for the 4th Duke by Sir William Chambers. It was here that Winston Churchill proposed to Clementine Hozier in 1908.

The temple was restored by the present Duke during European Architectural Heritage Year in 1975, when two plaques were unveiled by Lady Churchill to commemorate the event.

As the walk continues, it passes four incense cedars, each more than 15 metres (50 feet) high, towering above the yew and prunus. This area of the gardens also contains specimens of a number of other interesting rare trees, some said to be the first of their kind imported into Britain, and shrubs. The arboretum is particularly attractive in spring, when the blossom is out and the grassy banks are covered in daffodils and bluebells.

The Arboretum

The Rose Garden

To the right is the Rose Garden, encircled by a walkway and overarched by slender hoops covered in delicate pink climbing roses. At the centre of the garden is a circular bed with a statue, which is surrounded by symmetrical beds of roses in shades of red, pink and white. On the right of the Rose Garden is the Temple of Flora. Beyond this the path dips left towards giant cedars before bending right to reach the Grand Cascade. On the right a path passes an attractive clump of dogwood to join the lakeside walk.

Watercolour by Susan, Marchioness of Blandford (wife of the 5th Duke), Rosa chinensis semperflorens

Central statue in the Rose Garden

The Grand Cascade

The Temple of Diana

Designed by 'Capability' Brown in the 1760s, the Grand Cascade at the western end of the lake is one of England's most picturesque waterfalls. Here the Glyme plunges dramatically from the lake and then slowly winds south-westwards under the 'New' Bridge designed by Sir William Chambers, eventually joining the River Evenlode, a tributary of the Thames.

From the falls the path continues beside the lake and back towards the Palace. The boat house was built in 1888 for the 8th Duke and his second (American) Duchess, Lilian. On the gable facing the lakeside runs the inscription: "So may thy craft glide gently on as years roll down the stream."

- When the 5th Duke succeeded to the title in 1817 he was determined to create at Blenheim Palace "the finest botanical and flower garden in England". Over the years he introduced exotic grottoes and other rustic fantasies in the area around the Grand Cascade, inspired by the arrival in Britain of dozens of new varieties of plants from abroad. Although most of his additions have long since gone, the Swiss Bridge remains.

The Lake and the Bridge

When the 1st Duke and his architect Vanbrugh were planning the site for Blenheim Palace in Woodstock Park in 1705, it was clear that the proposed main approach would need to cross the wide, marshy valley of the Glyme stream and its tributaries.

The Rose Garden pergola

'Capability' Brown's Grand Cascade and the Swiss Bridge

Chambers' New Bridge   **Vanbrugh's Grand Bridge**

• "If these two lakes had been designed as one vast expanse of water, the effect would have been tedious," wrote Brown's biographer, Dorothy Stroud. "As it is they are united yet divided by Vanbrugh's bridge, from which the two parts spread out like the loops of a nicely tied bow."

• There is no evidence that Vanbrugh's bridge was ever lived in, although some of the rooms have fireplaces and chimneys. One even has an elliptical arch, perhaps for a theatre. Old guidebooks describe the bridge as a cool retreat and picnic venue in summer. Unfortunately, it is no longer safe to enter now.

Undeterred, Vanbrugh saw this marsh crossed by the finest bridge in Europe. The Duke duly approved his grand design and the bridge was begun in 1708. However, the construction posed significant engineering challenges. For instance, the huge chasms between the bridge and the sides of the valley had to be filled with tons of rubble from the ruins of Woodstock Manor and earth from the hill on which it had stood. Eventually, the main arch was keyed in 1710, measuring 31 metres (101 feet) wide.

The 1st Duchess claimed to a friend that she had counted 33 rooms in the bridge. In his defence, Vanbrugh assured her that if, when it was finished, she found a house inside it she could go and live in it!

Soon after the 1st Duke's death in 1722, Sarah asked his military engineer, Colonel Armstrong, to construct a formal canal-and-basin scheme, but this was swept away in 1764 when Lancelot 'Capability' Brown was commissioned to re-landscape Blenheim Palace. With one master-stroke, Brown gave a purpose to Vanbrugh's heroic Grand Bridge. He built a dam and cascade near Bladon, letting the Glyme run through the lower parts of the bridge, engulfing its ground floor, creating magnificent 'natural' lakes on either side and the picturesque remains of a causeway, known as Elizabeth's Island.

The visible height of the bridge is consequently a great deal less than Vanbrugh intended, especially as the arcaded superstructure that was planned to crown it was never built. Nevertheless, as Sir Sacheverell Sitwell remarked: "The lake at Blenheim is the one great argument of the landscape gardener. There is nothing finer in Europe."

The Palace and boathouse across 'Capability' Brown's lake

The Column of Victory

The 1st Duke in victory pose

The 41-metre (134-foot)-high Doric 'Column of Victory' stands at the entrance to the Great Avenue in the Park. It is crowned by a lead statue of the 1st Duke, by Robert Pit. The statue depicts him dressed as a Roman general, with eagles at his feet and a Winged Victory in his hand. The monument was begun in 1727, five years after his death, and completed in 1730 at a cost of £3,000.

The design and location of the monument were decided only after much deliberation by his widow, Duchess Sarah. She rejected various designs by Nicholas Hawksmoor and others, before calling in Lord Herbert and Roger Morris, the architect of the Palladian Bridge at Wilton, to complete the work.

The Duchess was also concerned about the Column's inscriptions. Three sides feature extracts from the Acts of Parliament that settled the estate on the 1st Duke and his descendants in both the male and female lines. On the fourth side, facing the palace, is an epitaph to Marlborough by Lord Bolingbroke (Henry St John) – ironically a hated political foe of the Marlboroughs from the days of Queen Anne. The Duchess had approached many different writers, including Alexander Pope, before finding that Lord Bolingbroke was the only man capable of rising to the challenge of commemorating the great Duke.

She described the epitaph he wrote as "the finest thing that was possible for any man to write and as often as I have read it I still wet the paper."

The Column of Victory. The base includes details of the 1st Duke's victories

- Sir Winston Churchill wrote of the Column of Victory's epitaph in his biography of the 1st Duke: "The inscription is a masterpiece of compact and majestic statement. In fact, it would serve as a history in itself, were all other records lost."

The Pleasure Gardens

The Pleasure Gardens have been created around the old, walled Kitchen Garden of the Palace, which now contains the Marlborough Maze.

The area still provides fresh fruit (including prizewinning grapes) and vegetables for the Palace, as well as hot-house flowers and shrubs, although it now also contains a number of attractions for the enjoyment of Blenheim Palace's visitors.

Giant chess and draughts games

Opposite the garden café is the Lavender Garden, with trellis walks and pergolas, walled in mellow brick. Other visitor attractions, in the maze area, include a scale model of part of Woodstock, putting greens, giant chess and draughts, an adventure play area and several two-dimensional maze puzzles. A narrow-gauge railway links the Palace to the Pleasure Gardens. The diesel locomotive, Sir Winston Churchill, pulls three canopied carriages and can reach a speed of 12mph.

The Butterfly House

Exotic tropical butterflies fly freely in the Butterfly House, which contains a special hatchery with the pupae of many species. Most butterflies live only a few weeks and over 100 tropical species are bred during the course of a season; so the butterflies you can see will vary from month to month.

The main flight section is virtually a 'natural' habitat where many of the plants are specially cultivated to provide food for the adult butterflies. It is possible to study the creatures' full life cycle here.

The attractive zebra finches exist happily with the butterflies and keep the area free from spiders' webs, a major threat to butterflies.

'Blenheim' at the centre of the Marlborough Maze

The Marlborough Maze

The Marlborough Maze is the world's second largest symbolic hedge maze – the lines of the hedges reflecting the splendour of the victory at Blenheim. Inspired by the trophies carved by Grinling Gibbons for the east and west colonnades of the Palace, the shapes include a giant cannon, cannonballs, trumpets and banners. The maze covers an area of 0.75 hectares (1.8 acres) and has two high wooden bridges that offer a perfect bird's eye view.

Special Events

Throughout the year Blenheim Palace provides a sumptuous backdrop for a full programme of events that reflect the changing seasons.

During the school holidays costumed entertainers provide an insight into the Palace's history through vivid storytelling.

As spring appears at Blenheim Palace, visitors can take part in special Easter events at the Pleasure Gardens and around the grounds.

Costumed entertainers at the Palace

Zara Phillips on Toytown winning the 'Europeans' in 2005

Jousting tournaments in late spring and summer see gallant knights and their mighty steeds meeting to battle for glory. These weekends are always packed with action and entertainment including falconry displays and knights charging in the traditional tilt and battling on foot.

As the days hot up for summer, there are many events to enjoy. Vintage car meetings take place in the grounds where visitors can marvel at the beautiful classic cars on display. Summer also sees craft fairs featuring quality goods from the finest craftsmen and women, and a variety of other sporting and special-interest events such as the Blenheim Palace Triathlon.

Jousting on the south lawn

The long summer nights at Blenheim Palace provide a wonderful opportunity for musical events and picnic-style concerts of classical music with a backdrop of fireworks.

In September equestrian fans can enjoy top-class sporting action at the International Horse Trials with the world's leading riders. There is plenty of excitement to keep everyone entertained, including an extensive retail village. Also in September Blenheim Palace hosts many of the Woodstock Literary Festival events, featuring numerous well known authors.

Vintage cars

As the nights draw in, the Palace looks to Christmas and becomes transformed into a winter wonderland providing a magical experience for visitors. Christmas trees sparkle in the colonnades, warm fires glow in the Palace and decorations adorn the elegant rooms. Visitors can enter into the festive spirit by visiting the Craft Fair, a perfect shopping opportunity for Christmas presents.

Blenheim Palace at Christmas

"We shape our buildings;
thereafter they shape us."

Sir Winston Churchill

The Dukes of Marlborough

John: First Duke

Henrietta: Second Duchess

Charles: Third Duke

George: Fourth Duke

George: Fifth Duke

George: Sixth Duke

John: Seventh Duke

George: Eighth Duke

Charles: Ninth Duke

Albert: Tenth Duke

John: Eleventh Duke

The Marlborough (Spencer-Churchill) line of descent

Sir Winston Churchill b. 1620 = ELIZABETH DRAKE of Ashe, Devon

John
b. 1650, cr. Duke of Marlborough*
and K.G. 1702
cr. Prince of the Holy Roman
Empire 1705. dspms. 16 June, 1722
= SARAH
dr. of Richard Jennings of St Albans
b. 1660. m. 1677/8 d. 1744

* Duke of Marlborough: a title which John Churchill
is believed to have taken in consequence of a
connection on his mother's side with the family of
Ley, Earls of Marlborough, extinct ten years previously.

JOHN
Marquess of
Blandford
b. 1686. d. 1703

Henrietta
b. 1681. Suc. as Duchess
of Marlborough 1722
dspms. 1733
= FRANCIS
2nd Earl of
Godolphin

ANNE
b. 1684
d. 1716
= CHARLES SPENCER
K.G., 3rd Earl of
Sunderland

ELIZABETH
b. 1687
d. 1714
= SCROOP
1st Duke of
Bridgewater

MARY
b. 1689
d. 1751
= JOHN
2nd Duke of
Montague

ROBERT SPENCER
b. 1701. Suc. as
Earl of Sunderland
1722. d. unm. 1729

Charles Spencer
b. 1706. Suc. as Earl of Sunderland 1729
and as 3rd Duke of Marlborough 1733.
K.G. d. 1758
= ELIZABETH
dr. of Baron
Trevor

JOHN SPENCER =
(Ancestor of the
Earls Spencer)
GEORGINA
dr. of
Earl Granville

DIANA SPENCER
b. 1708. d. 1735
= JOHN
4th Duke of
Bedford, K.G.

George Spencer
4th Duke of Marlborough
K.G., L.L.D., F.R.S.
b. 1739. Suc. 1758. d. 1817
= CAROLINE
dr. of Duke of Bedford
b. 1743. d. 1811

† The 5th Duke was authorised in 1817 to 'take and use the
name of Churchill, in addition to and after that of Spencer...
in order to perpetuate in His Grace's family a surname
to which his illustrious ancestor, John, first Duke of
Marlborough, added such imperishable lustre'.

George Spencer-Churchill†
5th Duke of Marlborough
b. 1766. Suc. 1817. d. 1840
= SUSAN
dr. of 7th Earl of Galloway
b. 1767. d. 1841

George Spencer-Churchill
6th Duke of Marlborough
b. 1793. Suc. 1840. d. 1857
= (i) JANE, dr. of 8th Earl of Galloway. d. 1844
(ii) CHARLOTTE, dr. of Viscount Ashbrook. d. 1850
(iii) JANE, dr. of Hon. Edward Stewart. d. 1897

John Winston Spencer-Churchill
7th Duke of Marlborough, K.G.
b. 1822. M.P. Suc. 1857
Gov. Gen. of Ireland 1876–80. d. 1883
= FRANCES
dr. of Marquess of Londonderry

George Charles Spencer-Churchill
8th Duke of Marlborough
b. 1844. Suc. 1883. d. 1892
= (i) ALBERTHA
dr. of Duke of Abercorn
(ii) LILIAN
dr. of Cicero Price (U.S.A.)

RANDOLPH HENRY SPENCER-CHURCHILL = JENNIE
b. at Blenheim 1849   dr. of Leonard Jerome (U.S.A.)
P.C., LL.D., etc. d. 1895   d. 1921

WINSTON LEONARD SPENCER-CHURCHILL = CLEMENTINE D.B.E.
K.G., O.M., C.H., M.P., etc. b. at Blenheim 30 Nov. 1874   dr. of Sir Henry Montagu
d. 24 Jan., 1965. Buried at Bladon, Oxon   Hozier, K.C.B. d. 12 Dec., 1977

**Charles Richard John
Spencer-Churchill**
9th Duke of Marlborough, K.G.
b. 1871. Suc. 1892. d. 1934
= (i) CONSUELO dr. of William Vanderbilt (U.S.A.)
m. 1895. d. 1964
(ii) GLADYS dr. of Edward Parker Deacon (U.S.A.)
m. 1921. d. 1977

**John Albert Edward William
Spencer-Churchill**
10th Duke of Marlborough, J.P., D.L.
b. 1897. Suc. 1934. d. 1972
= (i) ALEXANDRA MARY CADOGAN
dr. of Viscount Chelsea. m. 1920. C.B.E., J.P.
Chief Comdt. A.T.S. 1938–40. d. 1961
(ii) LAURA dr. of Hon. Guy Charteris. m. 1972

IVOR CHARLES SPENCER-CHURCHILL
b. 1898. d. 1956

**John George Vanderbilt
Henry Spencer-Churchill**
11th Duke of Marlborough. J.P., D.L.
b. 13 April, 1926. Suc. 1972
= (i) SUSAN MARY dr. of Michael Hornby
m. 1951. d. 2005
(ii) ATHINA MARY
dr. of Stavros G. Livanos
m. 1961
(iii) DAGMAR ROSITA. dr. of Count Carl
Ludwig Douglas. m. 1972
(iv) LILY MAHTANI m. 2008

CHARLES GEORGE
WILLIAM COLIN
SPENCER-CHURCHILL
b. 1940. m.
(i) 1965 Gillian
Spreckels Fuller
(ii) 1970 Elizabeth
Jane Wyndham

SARAH CONSUELO
SPENCER-CHURCHILL
b. 1921, d. 2000 m.
(i) 1943 Edwin F.
Russell (U.S.N.R)
(ii) 1966 Guy Burgos
(iii) 1967 Theodorous
Roubanis

CAROLINE
SPENCER-
CHURCHILL
b. 1923. m. 1946
Major Charles
Hugo Waterhouse.
d. 1992

ROSEMARY MILDRED SPENCER-CHURCHILL
b. 1929. m. 1953 Charles Robert Muir

JOHN DAVID IVOR
SPENCER-CHURCHILL
b. 1952. d. 1955

Charles James Spencer-Churchill
Marquis of Blandford.
b. 24 Nov., 1955
= (i) REBECCA MARY
FEW BROWN
m. 1990

(ii) EDLA GRIFFITHS
m. 2002

HENRIETTA MARY
SPENCER-CHURCHILL
b. 1958
m. 1980
NATHAN GELBER

RICHARD
SPENCER-
CHURCHILL
b. 1973. d. 1973

EDWARD ALBERT
CHARLES SPENCER-
CHURCHILL. b. 1974

ALEXANDRA
ELIZABETH MARY
SPENCER-
CHURCHILL. b. 1977

George John Godolphin Spencer-Churchill
Earl of Sunderland. b. 28 July, 1992

DAVID ABA GELBER
b. 1981

MAXIMILLIAN
HENRY GELBER
b. 1985

ARAMINTA CLEMENTINE MEGAN
CADOGAN SPENCER-CHURCHILL
b. 2007

CASPAR IVOR ELLIS SPENCER-CHURCHILL
b. 2008

dspms. = decessit sine prole mascula supersita, deceased with no surviving rightful male heirs

Further information

Opening times

The Palace, Park and Gardens will be open daily from mid February until end October, and Wednesdays to Sundays during November and until mid December. The Park opens from 9 am, the Formal Gardens from 10 am and the Palace at 10.30 am. Guided tours of the Palace available throughout the day. Private tours available to pre-booked groups. Last entry to the Palace and Park is at 4.45 pm. The Palace closes at 5.30 pm, and the Park and Gardens close at 6 pm.

During the Palace closed season, the Park remains open, except for Christmas Day, from 9 am until 4.45 pm or dusk.

Ticketing

Two types of daily tickets are available:

Palace, Park and Gardens

Access to all areas including the Palace, special exhibitions, the Park and Formal Gardens, shops, restaurants, the train and all attractions within the Pleasure Gardens.

Park and Gardens

Access to all areas as above except the Palace and the Winston Churchill Exhibition in the Palace.

Free Annual Pass

When you purchase a day ticket to the Palace (or upgrade a Park and Gardens ticket) you can convert it to an Annual Pass – for free! This allows unlimited entry to the public areas for a 12 month rolling period from time of purchase. Terms and Conditions apply.

Friends of Blenheim Palace Foundation Charity

This premium membership spends 100% of its income on the restoration of Blenheim Palace. It provides unlimited entry for a 12 month rolling period from the time of purchase, invitations to exclusive events, access to the Friend's Hospitality Lounge and 10% discount in our shops and cafes.

For more information and ticket prices visit www.blenheimpalace.com

Shopping

Unique shops provide an array of gifts, memorabilia and estate-produced food and beverages such as Blenheim Palace natural mineral water, honey and specially selected ranges of champagne, wines and liqueurs. The combination of books, toiletries, our new 'Below Stairs' range and gifts for the home and garden, inspired by the beautiful Palace and Grounds, make shopping at Blenheim Palace a delight.
Mail order service available.
Email: shop@blenheimpalace.com
Visit www.blenheimpalace.com for a selection of seasonal gifts.

Eating at the Palace

Enjoy an exciting selection of food in our cafes and restaurants. Freshly made sandwiches, cakes and pastries or a delicious hot meal with Blenheim Palace wines.

Banqueting, Weddings and Conferences

Delight your guests by hosting your event in one of our stunning rooms. Enjoy magnificent views and attentive, professional service that will give you a truly memorable occasion. Email: hospitality@blenheimpalace.com

Education

The Blenheim Palace Education Service offers a wide range of programmes on site for school, college and university students. We also offer an outreach programme and talks for groups and associations. Children's trails for the Park and Gardens can be downloaded free from our website or purchased from the Flagstaff gift shop.
www.blenheimpalace.com/education
Email: education@blenheimpalace.com

Further enquiries

Operations Department, Blenheim Palace, Woodstock, Oxfordshire OX20 1PX.
Tel: 01993 810530 or
0800 849 6500 - Free 24 hour recorded information
Fax: 01993 810 570
www.blenheimpalace.com

General information

Occasionally it is necessary for furniture, paintings or other exhibits to be moved; or for room layouts to be altered. Therefore items referred to in the guidebook may not be on display, or may be displayed in other settings.

The right to close the Park or Palace without notice is reserved.

Designed by Jamieson Eley

First published in 2012 by Hudson's Heritage Group, Peterborough PE3 6AG
Telephone 01733 296911
www.hudsonsheritage.com

Text by Paul Duffie, John Forster and Bernie Sheehan
All photographs in this book were taken by Peter Smith of Newbery Smith Photography and are © Hudson's Heritage Group with the exception of: Skyscan: cover, Blenheim Palace: p51, p53, p58 and p59 taken by Richard Cragg

Produced by Hudson's Heritage Group

ISBN: 978-0-7117-4229-1
Printed in Great Britain 92047 - 02/12